When I Was Young

HOME LIFE
IN THE 1930s AND 40s

HOME LIFE
IN THE 1930s and 40s

Faye Gardner with Joyce Williams

Evans

First published in this edition in 2012 by Evans Brothers Ltd
2A Portman Mansions
Chiltern St
London W1U 6NR

www.evansbooks.co.uk

British Library Cataloguing in Publication Data

Gardner, Faye.
Home life in the 1930s and 40s. — (When I was young)
1. Nineteen thirties—Juvenile literature. 2. Nineteen
forties—Juvenile literature. 3. Home economics—Great
Britain—History—20th century—Juvenile literature.
4. Great Britain—Social life and customs—20th century—
Juvenile literature.
I. Title II. Series III. Williams, Joyce.
941'.084-dc22

ISBN-13: 9780237543853

Acknowledgements

Planning and production by Discovery Books Limited
Edited by Faye Gardner
Commissioned photography by Alex Ramsay
Designed by Calcium

The publisher would like to thank Joyce Williams for her kind help in the preparation of this book.

For permission to reproduce copyright material, the author and publishers gratefully acknowledge the following: The Advertising Archive Limited: 24; the art archive: 15 (right); Hulton Getty: 14, 17 (top), 22-23 (top); Leominster Museum: 8, 11, 16, 24 (bottom); The Board of Trustees of the National Museuems and Galleries on Merseyside (Stewart Bale Archive): 12-13 (centre); The National Museum of Wales: cover, 9 (top), 12 (left), 20, 21 (top), 27 (bottom), 28; The Robert Opie Collection: 13 (right), 15 (left), 17 (bottom), 18, 19, 22 (bottom), 23 (bottom), 25, 26, 27 (top); Rural History Centre, University of Reading: 10 (top); Shropshire County Museum Service: 9 (bottom).

Contents

Family and home 6

Jobs on the farm 8

Getting about 10

Wartime visitors 12

Heating the house 14

Washing and bathing 16

Doing the laundry 18

Going to the market 20

Rationing 22

Baking bread and cakes 24

Storing food 26

Busy days 28

Glossary 29

Useful books and websites 29

Activities and cross-curricular work 30

Index 32

'Life on our farm was hard.'

My name is Joyce and I love meeting up with my family. This is Ellie who is twelve and Hannah who is eight.

I was born in 1934, before the Second World War. When I was young, I lived on a farm near a small town called Knighton in Wales. The picture below shows you how the town looked then. My dad was a farmer and my mum was a housewife. I had a younger sister called Ruth to play with. Our grandparents lived on another farm nearby.

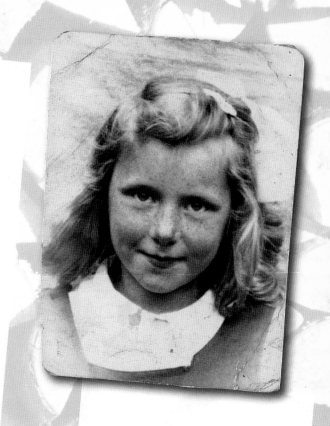

Life on our farm was hard. We didn't have tractors or machines to help us with the work. We were always very busy. I am going to tell you about our home and what life was like then.

'My sister and I helped on the farm.'

On our farm we kept sheep, pigs, cows and chickens. We grew **grain** and vegetable crops, too. We lived in a long-house, which was built out of stone.

The long-house was split into two parts: we lived in one half and in the winter the animals lived in the other.

My sister and I helped on the farm. Ruth milked the cows and I collected the eggs from the hens. At **harvest** time we helped pick the potatoes and swede. Every summer there was haymaking in the fields. We used long rakes and pitchforks to pile the loose hay into haystacks. The hay was used to feed the animals in the winter.

'We walked everywhere'

We didn't have a car because they were too expensive. We walked everywhere, or went in a pony and trap like this one. Ruth and I had to walk five miles (8km) to school and back every day. This is what our school looks like today.

Parish Church, Knighton

Before and after school, we had to help Mum in the house. We worked on Saturdays too, but had a day off on Sundays. We were still busy though, because we had to go to church in Knighton three times! In the evening Mum and Dad took us in the pony and trap, but the other two times we had to walk. That meant we walked twelve miles (19km) altogether. I was very fit when I was young.

'An evacuee came to live with us.'

During the war, an **evacuee** called Jack came to live with us. He was from Liverpool. His parents sent him to the countryside because the city was being badly bombed. This is how Liverpool looked then.

Jack liked to play with the lambs on our farm.

The war forced many men to leave their families to fight in the **armed forces**. My dad stayed at home because he was a farmer. Farmers were needed to grow food for the rest of the country to eat.

A lot of jobs on the farms were done by women who worked for the **Women's Land Army**. Two women called Gwynne and Mary came to work on our farm.

For a healthy, happy job

Join the
WOMEN'S
LAND
ARMY

for details:
APPLY TO NEAREST W.L.A. COUNTY OFFICE OR TO W.L.A. HEADQUARTERS 6 CHESHAM PLACE LONDON S.W.1
STREET

'We went to bed by candlelight.'

The house was cold in winter, because we didn't have central heating. I slept in the same bed as my sister to keep warm! Most of the rooms had an open fireplace in which we burned wood to heat the house.

The living room was my favourite place because it had a huge fireplace. It was the only room that was warm and cosy.

We lit paraffin heaters in the rooms that did not have a fireplace. The paraffin smelt horrible and made the walls very damp. Sometimes the wallpaper fell off!

There were no electric lights in our house. We used oil lamps in the evenings and went to bed by candlelight. My sister and I used to go upstairs together because it was so dark and spooky.

'We got our water from a pump outside.'

Our house did not have running water. We got our water from this pump outside.

My granddad used to get water from this pump, too.

Most people did not have toilets or bathrooms inside their houses. We washed at the kitchen sink downstairs and had a bath in the kitchen, too!

Our toilet was in a shed at the bottom of the garden. It was not very nice. There were two holes in the ground and a little wooden seat to sit on. It was very cold in the winter! We used to cut up old newspapers into small squares for toilet paper.

'Everything had to be washed by hand.'

Mum always did the washing on a Monday. There were no washing machines, so everything had to be washed by hand. We scrubbed the clothes on a **washboard** to get them clean.

THEN A NEIGHBOUR TOLD ME TO TRY FAIRY FOR MY WASHING. IT'S WONDERFUL! MILD, BUT THOROU~~G~~

The clothes were squeezed through a mangle to get the water out. Then they were hung on a line outside, or in front of the fire to dry.

Ironing was hard work, too. We didn't have an electric iron. Instead we used flat irons, which were heated on top of a **range** in the kitchen.

I ironed the clothes on a big blanket on top of the kitchen table. My arms used to ache because the irons were so heavy.

'The streets were full of stalls.'

Thursday was shopping day and my favourite day of the week. It was market day in Knighton and Dad took us there in the pony and trap. The streets were full of stalls selling fruit and vegetables.

The farmers brought their animals to sell at the cattle market. Most of the farmers did not have lorries or vans. They had to walk the animals down the roads with their sheepdogs. There was always a lot of shouting and whistling!

Every September some of our sheep were sold at the market. I used to help Dad walk them to town. It was my job to run ahead and open the gates in the fields to let the sheep through.

'Everyone was given a ration book.'

During the war there was not enough food in the shops and some things had to be **rationed**. We could only buy a certain amount of meat and other foods each week. People spent a lot of time queuing for food.

Everyone had a **ration book** which said how much food they could buy. The food rations in this picture would have to last one person for a whole week.

My family was lucky because we could get food from our farm. We always had plenty to eat. It was harder for people in cities to get fresh food.

DIG FOR VICTORY

For their sake —
GROW YOUR OWN
VEGETABLES

The government encouraged families with gardens to grow their own vegetables. They put up posters like this one.

'The cooking was done on the kitchen range.'

Every Friday Mum made bread and cakes. The cooking was done on the kitchen range.

On one side of the range there was a **boiler** which heated our water, and on the other there was an oven for baking.

There was a fire in the middle of the range where we burned small logs to make it hot. We used the bellows you can see on the wall to make the fire burn up. We had to wait nearly two hours before the oven was hot enough to bake the bread.

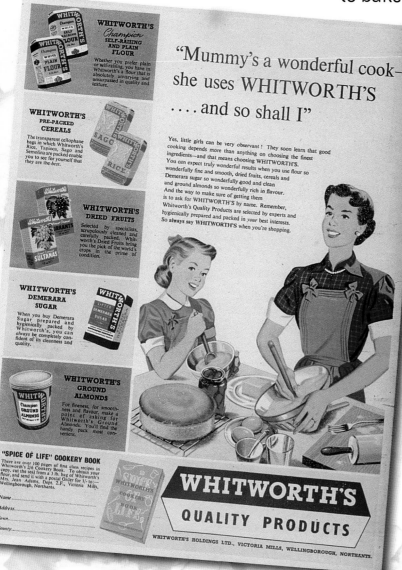

Sometimes Mum baked currant buns as a treat. The kitchen was always nice and warm on a Friday. It smelt good, too!

'We didn't have a fridge.'

We didn't have a fridge or freezer to keep the food in. We had a huge cupboard called a pantry. It was so big you could walk around inside. It had lots of wooden shelves to store the food on and the floor was made of stone to keep it cool.

There were metal hooks in the beams in the ceiling from which we hung big pieces of meat. Sometimes we covered the meat and vegetables with salt to make them last longer. This stopped the food from going bad but it made everything taste salty! My grandma used to help my mum salt the bacon.

SAXA Salt

UNTOUCHED BY HAND FROM BRINE WELL TO SEALED PACKAGE

Obtainable at All Grocers and Stores

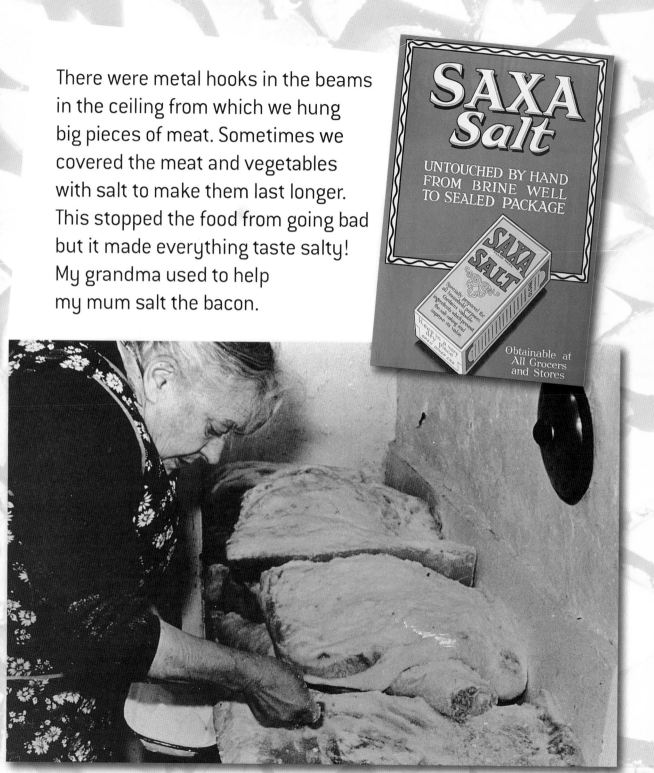

'We enjoyed ourselves.'

When I was young, we didn't have much spare time for hobbies or relaxing. We were too busy with the housework and farmwork.

But we enjoyed ourselves all the same.

Glossary

Armed forces The army, navy and airforce.

Boiler A tank in which water is heated.

Evacuee Someone who was moved from a city made dangerous by bombing, to a safer place in the countryside.

Grain A seed crop, like wheat or barley.

Harvest The time of year when ripe crops are picked.

Range An oven heated by wood or coal.

Ration To limit the amount of something that people are allowed when it is in short supply.

Ration book A book of tickets used by people to buy rations.

Washboard A wooden or metal board with ridges that is used for scrubbing clothes.

Women's Land Army A force of young women who worked on farms to replace the men who had joined the armed forces.

Useful books and websites

There are lots of books to read and websites to visit to learn more about home life in the 1930s and 40s. Here are a few to get you started:

www.bbc.co.uk/schools/primaryhistory/world_war2/wartime_homes
Read about wartime homes, with fun activities and quizzes.

www.movinghistory.ac.uk/homefront/themes/homefamilylife.html
Watch clips from footage of daily life.

www.bbc.co.uk/london/content/image_galleries/
1940s_house_gallery.shtml?1
Look at photographs of a reconstructed house from the 1940s.

Britain since 1930 (Britain through the Ages), Stewart Ross, Evans 2003
Evacuation (At Home in World War Two), Stewart Ross, Evans 2003
Rationing (At Home in World War Two), Stewart Ross, Evans 2003

Activities and cross-curricular work

Activities suggested on this page support progression in learning by consolidating and developing ideas from the book and helping the children to link the new concepts with their own experiences. Making these links is crucial in helping young children to engage with learning and to become lifelong learners.

Ideas on the next page develop essential skills for learning by suggesting ways of making links across the curriculum and in particular to literacy, numeracy and ICT.

Word Panel
Check that the children know the meaning of each of these words and ideas from the book, in addition to the words in the glossary.

- Afterwards
- Ago
- Before
- Bombs/ bombing
- Cattle
- Church
- Crops
- Flat iron
- Mangle
- Market day
- Oil lamps
- Open fireplace
- Paraffin heaters
- Pitchforks
- Second World War
- Water pump

Research Questions
Once you have read and discussed the book, ask groups of children to talk together and think of more information they would like to know. Can they suggest where to look for the answers?

Being a Historian
Discuss how we know about things that happened in the past.

- Check that children have an understanding of the idea of 'past'. A large scale timeline can be helpful. Get a long roll of paper and use 1 metre to represent 10 years. So starting with the present day, go back in decades until you reach the 1930s.
- Ask children to find out when they, their parents, their grandparents and their great grandparents were born. Mark these dates on the timeline.
- Can the children find family photographs from each of those times? These can be added to the timeline. Explain that these are evidence of how people dressed and things that they had at the time.
- Prepare children to interview older generations in their families. Agree what you want to find out: clothing, vehicles, washing, lighting, toys etc and help children to prepare a questionnaire. This is another form of evidence historians use: eye witness accounts.
- Ask children to think of other sources of evidence they can use to add more information to their timeline (e.g. books in a library, pictures on the internet; news programmes available to schools online; contemporary newspapers).

Keeping Food
Ask children to research all the ways food in their houses is kept safe to eat. Suggest they consider: freezing, keeping cold, canning, drying, salting, smoking, cooking, wrapping.

- Find information in the book about how food was kept from rotting.
- Keep some food in wrapped in plastic in a warm place in the classroom and allow it to go bad (e.g. bread, cucumber, fruit) but beware of health and safety, particularly mould spores for children with asthma.
- Keep a food diary recording the feel and look of the food. Use digital cameras to record the way the food looks.
- Discuss why some methods of food preservation were not used in the 1930s. Find out how food was stored in the 1930s.

Keeping Healthy
Ask children to reread the book considering whether Joyce was a healthy child. Then ask them to consider why.

- Compare what they know of Joyce's daily routines to their own. Consider
  - Exercise
  - Diet
  - Leisure activities.
- Talk about why these have changed over the years, and whether all of the changes have made life better for children.

Using 'Home Life in the 1930s and 40s' for cross-curricular work.

The web below indicates some areas for cross-curricular study. Others may well come from your own class's engagement with the ideas in the book.

The activities suggested will help children to develop key competencies as:

- successful learners
- confident individuals and
- responsible citizens.

Cross-curricular work is particularly beneficial in developing the thinking and learning skills that contribute to building these competencies because it encourages children to make links, to transfer learning skills and to apply knowledge from one context to another. As importantly, cross-curricular work can help children to understand how school work links to their daily lives. For many children, this is a key motivation in becoming a learner.

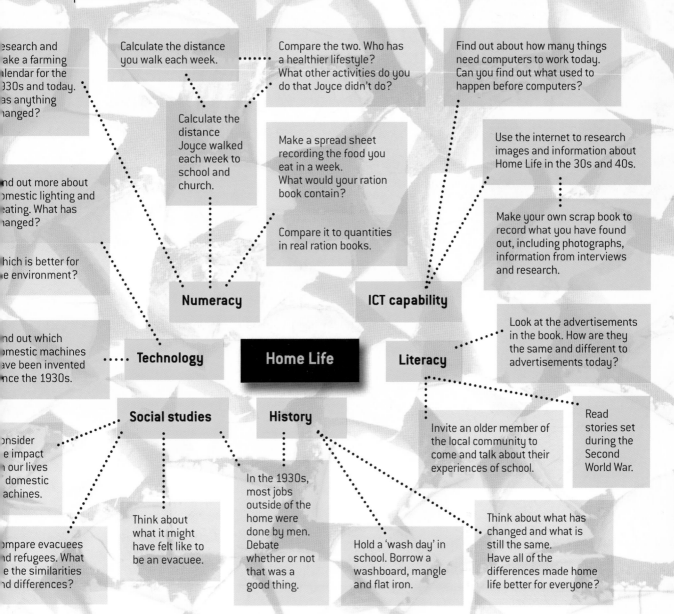

...search and ...ake a farming ...alendar for the ...930s and today. ...as anything ...anged?

Calculate the distance you walk each week.

Compare the two. Who has a healthier lifestyle? What other activities do you do that Joyce didn't do?

Find out about how many things need computers to work today. Can you find out what used to happen before computers?

Calculate the distance Joyce walked each week to school and church.

Make a spread sheet recording the food you eat in a week. What would your ration book contain?

Use the internet to research images and information about Home Life in the 30s and 40s.

...nd out more about ...omestic lighting and ...eating. What has ...anged?

Compare it to quantities in real ration books.

Make your own scrap book to record what you have found out, including photographs, information from interviews and research.

...hich is better for ...e environment?

Numeracy

ICT capability

...nd out which ...omestic machines ...ave been invented ...nce the 1930s.

Technology

Home Life

Literacy

Look at the advertisements in the book. How are they the same and different to advertisements today?

Social studies

History

Invite an older member of the local community to come and talk about their experiences of school.

Read stories set during the Second World War.

...onsider ...e impact ...n our lives ...domestic ...achines.

Think about what it might have felt like to be an evacuee.

In the 1930s, most jobs outside of the home were done by men. Debate whether or not that was a good thing.

Hold a 'wash day' in school. Borrow a washboard, mangle and flat iron.

Think about what has changed and what is still the same. Have all of the differences made home life better for everyone?

...ompare evacuees ...nd refugees. What ...e the similarities ...nd differences?

Index

baking 24, 25
bathing 17

cars 10
church 11
cooking 24, 25

Dad 7, 11, 13, 20, 21

evacuees 12

farm animals 8, 9, 12, 21
farm work 7, 8, 9, 11, 13, 21
food 20, 22, 23, 24, 25, 26, 27

grandparents 7, 16, 27

heating 14, 15

ironing 19

lighting 15

markets 20, 21
Mum 7, 11, 18, 24, 25

oven 24, 25

pantry 26, 27
pony and trap 10, 11, 20

range 24, 25
rationing 22, 23

school 10, 11
shopping 20, 22, 23
sister 7, 9, 10, 11, 14, 15

toilets 17
transport 10, 11, 20, 21

washing 17
washing clothes 18, 19
water pumps 16
Women's Land Army 13